The Atlas Of My Heart

My Poetry Book

Saraswatula Sai Srinidhi

BookLeaf
Publishing

India | USA | UK

Made with ❤ on the BookLeaf Publishing Platform
www.bookleafpub.in
www.bookleafpub.com

Dedication

I dedicate this book to my family and friends, who have inspired to get into poem writing. I enjoy every moment of this beautiful task.

Preface

It was just another balmy day in Singapore. I was seven years old, sitting in my room and had nothing to do. As time passed, I got even more bored. All I did was gaze out of the window. A while later, my father walked in. He saw me sitting there, with nothing to do. So, he told me to write a poem. I had no idea how I was supposed to do that. Poetry seemed like a very complicated task to me. My father told me to just write about any random topic. So, I sat down at the computer, immersed in thoughts. The best topic for me at that time was nature- the beautiful plants and the mesmerising scene outside my window. So, I started typing about everything I saw, everything I felt. My mother came by too and gave me a few tips. And in no time, the words started flowing out of my heart and onto the computer like music. Since then, I've always enjoyed the art of poetry.

Acknowledgements

I've learnt that poetry is a free art- you can write about anything you like, as long as it's from your heart.

1. The rhythm of the feet

Dance is the way I feel alive,
Something that makes my heart
thrive.

Sometimes the steps can seem
too rough
With practice, it is never tough.

But if you practice and give it
time,
The rhythm flows like a nursery
rhyme.

Dance can be limited, restricted and tight,
Or unlimited, open and bright.

It has many moods and changing grace,
But never a moment when it fades.

Melody or not, dance has its own charm,
From careful steps to an opened arm.

It has existed since the start of time,

With instruments that play and
bells that chime.

It doesn't have an end,
To me, it's an eternal friend.

Dance isn't just an art,
It's the language of the heart.

Something that's a part of me,
Which is always meant to be.

2. The vibrance of our world

Colours give everything a charm,
Like red for love and even harm.

The vibrant world of different
shades,
Where colours brighten and light
fades.

How could we recognise a tree,
for example,
If it weren't always so lusciously
green?

Or how would we describe a
building,
Without colours even after it's
seen?

In deepest shade and sudden
light,
They dress the world in dark and
bright.

In all their shades the colours
dance,
And catch my eye with every
glance.

With hue and tone, a gentle
sway,
They banish grey and start the
day.

An endless saga I could sing,
Of all the joy that colours bring.

3. My eternal light

Oh God, please bless my
everyday,
And put all my troubles at bay.
I'm grateful for the love you give,
For without it I wouldn't live.

You made the stars, You made the
sky,
You set the planets up so high.
You placed the grass, You grew
the trees,

You gave them all a touch of
breeze.

Every prayer of mine You hear,
And with Your light I have no
fear.
You give me hope, You give me
grace.
Every bit of your love I embrace.

I'm closer to You day by day,
And leave my worldly things
away.
You shield me with Your care- so
strong,

And tell me what's right and
what's wrong.

You're like a mother, kind and
pure,
To every problem You're the cure.
Whenever I need You, You're
there.
You're in me, near me and
everywhere.

Like a father You are too,
I see his strictness dwell in You.
But without it where would I be?

The right path, how would I then see?

I can't express my love for You,
You dwell inside my heart, it's true.
For in every moment You're there,
With Your infinite love and care.

4. Life-long companions

A time that starts but will not
cease,
A golden time that brings us
peace.

When needed, they are there to
guide,
To play, enjoy and crazy ride.

Leaving a friend,
Feels like the end.

They are the ones who make
days bright,
To dear companions, I give my
light.

When you don't expect one near,
The perfect friend will then
appear.

5. Love lives here

Is a home just filled with bricks
and stone?
Is it a place where you won't feel
alone?

Or is there something more to it?
Am I still unaware of it?

To me a home isn't just rooms
and walls,
It's a place filled with love that
enthrals.

With the tender feeling in the air,
Gives the house a charming flair.

It's a place where new memories
are sown,
A place I know is truly my own.

6. The hidden costs of progress

As our modern times took over
the Earth,
Everything started to grow,
But the natural grow of the
Earth,
Started growing too slow.

We started ruining the Earth,
By making our lives easier,
The nature started to perish,
From year to year.

Today we have technology,
But many things we've also lost,
It's the beauty of the nature,
That's what our comfort has cost.

7. What makes us special

Every soul is special in its own
way,
Each one shines a bit more every
day.

The things we've achieved
doesn't show who we entirely
are,
It's the love that we hold that's
seen from realms afar.

It could be about what we've
learned recently,
But surely about what's been
with us from the start- pure and
beautifully.

Grades, money, jobs and
smartness don't truly define what
makes us special,
It's the love, care and friendship
that grows in our potential.

Having the ability to dream and
look forward is the biggest gift
ever,

Because gifts like these will stay
with you forever.

Everyone has a special moment
to shine,
You have one and I have mine.

Though we just have to wait for
that moment to arrive,
The moment that which makes
us feel so alive.

It is our choices that show who
we truly are, far more than our
abilities

-Albus Dumbledore (Harry Potter)

8. The most misunderstood word

True beauty- the most
misunderstood thing ever,
Has this generation understood
this word?- Never.

Today beauty is defined by
colour, grandeur and jewellery.
But it's true meaning is a spark in
the heart that sets you free.

True beauty lies within,

Not in the texture of the hair or
the tone of the skin.

The help one freely offers to
others in times of need,
Are the ones who truly succeed.

No matter how gorgeous a
person would be,
It's the behaviour one would
clearly see.

A kind-hearted person may win
your heart,
Just because his or her words are
as sweet as apple-tart.

External beauty is important-
there's no denying that,
Though internal beauty is even
more important-the thing we
should look at.

9. Art by God

I wake up to a sparrow chirping
by my window,
With the soft, lusciously green
grass below.

The warm rays of the sun pour
into my room,
Which removes all the darkness
and the gloom.

I take a moment to breathe the
fresh air just outside,

And to admire the way the birds
glide.

The golden sun looks graciously
upon me,
And I gaze back at its rays with
such glee.

The wide blue sky with clouds so
fluffy and white,
In different shapes, both heavy
and light.

The vibrant flowers and the
buzzing bees,
The soft wind and the tall trees.

I sit there and admire God's
creativity,
Enjoying the sound of nature and
its vibrancy.

That little time spent was as
precious as gold,
As I get up and get ready for the
day to unfold.

10. The cry of the sky

Everybody has shed some tears,
Did you know the sky sheds
them too?
It's the weather on gloomy days,
None other than the rain that
pours on you.

On some days, the sky looks
depressed,
Though we may never know
why.

It's the beauty of emotions
hidden,
Way up high.

Sometimes the sky isn't in the
best mood,
It looks all grey, dull and sad.
They echo our own darkest days,
Days for us that we call bad.

But after a while,
These moments pass away,
And the sky is back to normal,
With the sun smiling brightly
today.

11. The language in silence

A pause taken after every
sentence,
A secret you wished to convey,
With a glance or a gesture,
But something you couldn't say.

The silence that pierces through
the ears,
A moment given to think,
To contemplate the meaning of a
gesture,

Be it a wave or a wink.

A subtle reaction is sufficient,
To show you've understood,
What the person was trying to
convey,
Was all clear as it stood.

12. I know you

I have written this poem for you,
Even if I might not even know
you.

But even without any knowledge,
I'm sure,
That you're a kind-hearted and
person with a heart so pure.

You have the spirit of a warrior,
plain to see.

With a heart as soft as a person
could be.

You're a caring person,
incomparably kind,
With sweet words and a perfectly
sharp mind.

Always believe in yourself no
matter how hard things get,
For with a positive attitude all
will be set.

Don't try to be someone you
aren't, you're perfect the way you
are,

I can tell that the beauty within
you can be seen from realms afar

.

Keep going forward soaring
through the sky,
Don't ever give up, just keep
flying high.

13. The emotions of nature

Nature has feelings too,
Its mood changes just like you.

Sometimes it's happy, angry or
sad,
And that's when the weather is
either good or bad.

When the sky shines with a
vibrant blue,
It looks all perfect, happy and
new.

When the sky sometimes turns
gloomy and cries,
One can feel the sadness pouring
from its eyes.

A sneeze it gives once a year,
Showers snow that's fluffy and
clear.

But if all of nature is active and
alright,
The flowers and leaves will spark
with light.

14. A fight with procrastination

When I feel lethargic, bored and
tired,
Though I still feel the pressure of
work,
I say "I can finish my work later",
A common, foolish quirk.

As the clock ticks by, bit by bit,
And time dances through the
day,
As nightfall covers the sky,

And the sunlight fades away.

But suddenly I snap upright,
And escape my lethargy in fear,
I've lost my time, I've lost it all,
Why didn't I do it earlier?

Anxiety and stress cloud my
head,
As I work late at my table,
I should have finished work in
the morning,
When I was fit and able.

I've learned my lesson, I've
understood my mistake
I won't do it again,
For time is precious, it won't
come back,
I won't let another day go in
vain.

15. Find X

This one alphabet can change
your entire life,
Its complexity acts like a sharp
knife.

Only a pragmatic person can
solve this mystery,
And if not- misery will cloud you
all throughout history.

Once it enters your life, stop
expecting better,

As from your 6th grade,
Your only problem will be this
one letter.

Only cerebral people can win this
battle,
If intellect is used you can win
the semester,
For this creature only wants your
awareness,
And may I remind you that it's a
pesky little prankster.

To some people it might just look
eccentric but manageable,

But to some its darkness will
look invincible.
Think of it as a real human,
But it's just a bit taciturn,

Though in its subject it's a
flamboyant celebrity,
Before tackling don't forget to
learn.

But not to fear- there's always
some brightness in everything,
For out of joy and cleverness,
you shall realise its true meaning

16. The boredom beast

A vicious monster thrives
amongst us,
Ready to devour time,
It's poison fills the mind with
boredom,
And traps us in a sticky slime.

Everyday we do some work,
But still our time feels thin,
This is when the monster strikes,
And lets the boredom in.

Boredom clouds our heads like
dust,
We don't know what to do,
But the monster enjoys this
frustration,
Eating the ideas left in you.

The only way to save ourselves,
Is to keep the mind at work,
For lazying around is just
Another foolish lurk.

17. The most vibrant subject

A subject with a world full of
integer flurries,
To some it's a joy while to others
it causes worries.

I sit there wondering how it
came to be,
For it's just the beauty the of
math that I see.

From the basics it soars way up
high,

To finding X- a problem, we cry!

The subject is filled with perfect
of logic,
Just understand it a bit and it
works like magic.

From formulas to terms, from
circles to squares,
From shapes to angles and
money affairs.

This world of math is yet a
mystery,
A vibrant subject- shining
throughout history.

18. Comes once but is gone forever

Time- something beyond all of

us,

We mark it by minutes and

hours,

Such a mysterious entity flows

throughout our day,

With the most extraordinary

powers.

Imagine what life would be,

Without a single measure of value,

How long did I study? How long did I dance?
Was it enough? I wish I knew.

Time and tide wait for none,
We know this saying: Time is grand.

Every moment is truly precious,
Every tick of the clock's hand.

Time is infinite, around us all,
It passes but never comes back,

So don't waste it, use it wisely,

For one day it will time that you lack.

19. The spark in the dark

Everyday thoughts cloud my
head,
And follow me straight to my
bed,
I overthink and I shed tears,
Worrying about my daily fears.

Stress and sadness follow me,
And wipe away my usual glee,
My stomach squirms with pain
inside,

For all these feelings I must hide.

Cold sweat trickles down my
face,
And my heartbeat starts to race,
Blood rushes through my ears so
fast,
And traps me in my painful past.

I try to breath and meditate,
And stop worrying about my
fate,
I raise myself from the painful
dark,
And within I ignite a spark.

I think about what makes my
day,
And put all my bad thoughts at
bay,
Soon I feel myself again,
And rise above the suffer and
pain.

20. The jewels up high

When the sunlight starts to fade,
And is covered in a dark shade,

The millions of stars smile at me,
And I return their gentle glee.

I gaze at the stars so high,
So elegant in the night sky.

They guide those who are
seeking light,
Their presence is forever bright.

They add a sparkle to the
darkness,
The endless sky they gently
dress.

When it's late and time to sleep,
I drift off to slumbers deep.

21. The subconscious zoo

I lie down, tired on my bed,
With thoughts swimming inside
my head,
Suddenly I see something weird,
Myself with a long, shiny beard.

I stare at myself, laughing mad,
I don't know why I didn't feel
sad.
Having a beared seemed pretty
fun,

So I tried to tie it in a bun.

But then I saw myself on mars,
Riding pigs instead of cars,
I joined the game and played
along,
With me singing a piggy song.

But soon everything changed so
fast,
Right next to me- a green bomb
blast,
I ran to save my dear hide,
With no time left for me to bide.

Something was ringing beside
me,
Something which I couldn't see,
I fought the sound with all my
might,
And yearned for the return of
night.